POEMS FOR VOICES

POEMS FOR VOICES

Al Purdy

Margaret Atwood

John Newlove

Phyllis Gotlieb

Tom Marshall

Alden Nowlan

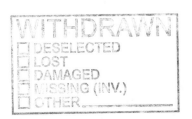
CANADIAN BROADCASTING CORPORATION, TORONTO

iNTRODUCTION

The "poems for voices" in this book were
commissioned for CBC radio's literary series
"Anthology", and were first broadcast in February
and March, 1970. They are to be broadcast a second
time on "Anthology" in late August and September,
1970.

The principle on which the commissions were made
was a simple and even subjective one. Some
Canadian poets — Earle Birney, for example, and
more recently Gwendolyn MacEwen — have written
radio drama or dramatic poems for radio. It seemed
to me that there were other poets who might be
interested in experimenting with dramatic themes
and the use of more than a single voice, and it then
seemed a good idea to approach a group of poets
whose published work made it more than likely that
anything they might write for radio would be of a
very distinctive nature. Six poets were approached,
all of them accepted the commission, and here are
the poems they wrote.

As for the poets:

A. W. Purdy lives in Ameliasburg, Ontario. His books
of poetry include *Poems for All the Annettes, The
Cariboo Horses* (Governor General's Award for
poetry for 1965), and *Wild Grape Wine*. He is also
the editor of *The New Romans*, an anthology of
"candid Canadian opinions" about the United
States.

Margaret Atwood has lived in many parts of Canada
and for the past two years in Edmonton. Her books
of poetry include *The Circle Game* (Governor
General's Award for poetry for 1966), *The Animals
in That Country*, and *The Journals of Susanna
Moodie*, a long poem first published on
"Anthology" in 1969 and available as a CBC poetry
recording. Miss Atwood is working on a movie script
based on her novel *The Edible Woman*.

Phyllis Gotlieb was born and still lives in Toronto. She has published a science fiction novel *Sunburst* and a novel set in Southern Ontario, *Why Should I Have All the Grief?* Her books of poetry are *Within the Zodiac* and *Ordinary, Moving*.

John Newlove was born in Regina and now lives in Terrace, B.C. He has published a half dozen books of poetry, including *Moving in Alone, Black Night Window* and *The Cave*. A long poem "The Pride" has been broadcast several times by the CBC.

Tom Marshall was born in Niagara Falls and teaches English at Queen's University in Kingston, Ontario. He edits the literary magazine "Quarry" and the small publishing firm Quarry Press. A book of his poetry *The Silences of Fire* was published in 1969.

Alden Nowlan was born in Nova Scotia and now lives in Fredericton, New Brunswick, where he is poet-in-residence at the University of New Brunswick. His books include *Bread, Wine and Salt* (Governor General's Award for poetry for 1967), *Wind in a Rocky Country*, and *The Mysterious Naked Man*. He has also published a collection of short stories, *Miracle at Indian River*.

The broadcasts of the poems were produced for "Anthology" by Ramona Randall in Montreal, Bill Terry in Vancouver, and Terence Gibbs and Alex Smith in Toronto.

Robert Weaver
July, 1970

vi

CONTENTS

The Myth Includes/Al Purdy

Oratorio For Sasquatch, Man, And Two Androids/Margaret Atwood

Notes From And Among The Wars/John Newlove

Doctor Umlaut's Earthly Kingdom/Phyllis Gotlieb

Words For An Imaginary Future/Tom Marshall

Gardens Of The Wind/Alden Nowlan

"THE MYTH INCLUDES..."

Al Purdy

Sound: *Motor car, fade down background after first line, out with train*

Middle-aged:

The red Ford squirts down the road like a grapefruit
seed going seventy miles an hour
thru all the northern towns I passed years ago,
or some other self died during the myth of youth,
a dream of trains in Northern Ont.
For this is a journey and I am the traveller,
moving from point A to point B,
alone inside a red bug,
moving west at night—
So tired the headlights probe between shadows
instead of destroying them,
leaving the solid blackness untouched
on either side of the road,
as the arriving past and future are untouched
—and this small bright area
I carry with me in my head
is now and glides between dark shadows,
between towns strung with beaded lights,
beyond the by-pass and the white line
on the highway I must not cross—
Sudbury, Espanola, Blind River and the Soo,
Wawa, Hawk Junction—Hawk Junction?
—where another self before the war
rode the jostling box cars west,

Sound: *Whistle of old-fashioned coal-burner locomotive*
became a boy criminal pursued
by train crew and the railway cop,

Sound: *Panting breath*

Middle-aged:

lost two days in the Algoma bush,
trying to locate a soul inside the wilderness—

Younger self:

Question: Are you afraid?
Answer: No, I'm not!
Another answer: wrong, you're scared shitless—
It's home and my own bed I want.
But it's warm weather for early fall,
and even lost I'm not quite witless,
despite the dark woods of Northern Ont.
Besides, I don't believe I'm lost!

Sound: *Chorus of animals, crows, owl hoots, etc. cut off leaving echoing silence*

Younger self:

(DEFIANT) I don't believe I'm lost!
I'm too intelligent for that,
but maybe I'd better pray a little
just in case: if God is not,
then it won't matter,
but might be handy if he is,
for take no chances, that's my motto—

Sound: *voice changes to man, like the sound of adolescent whose voice is changing to man, till end of this scene*

Younger voice:

Is this me, this boy
stumbling thru underbrush in Algoma,
that's too wet to build a fire?
Circling around inside himself,
new-born fossil remnant,
imperfect mammal wanting mamma,
homo sapiens in a diaper?

Sound: *Far-off trains. Fade down and out*

Sound: *Brief music*

Younger voice:
(STILL CHANGING) (TERRIFIED) But I could leave my bones here,
only a couple of miles from the village,
and no one would know or care,
the lighted place in my head extinguished—

Older voice:
(SLIGHTLY WEARY) Is there always an answer to being lost?
Well, in this case, the answer is a river
that crosses the railway line at Hawk Junction—

Younger voice:
(RESENTFUL) Is that so? Is that so?
Then why didn't you tell me before?

Older voice:
(DERISION) You didn't ask,
you green thought in a green shade—

Younger voice:
Okay, if you're so smart, make the sun shine
and the birds sing in these woods!

Older voice:
Listen—they're singing, it's shining—

Sound: *Faint birds*

Younger voice:
Why didn't they sing before?

Older voice:
You'd sing too if you'd just had breakfast.
In the meantime, take ten giant steps north

until you reach the river,
then four dwarf steps east to the village—

Music: *Brief, a few bars*

Middle-aged:
The red Ford goes down the road like
a grapefruit seed squirting seventy
miles an hour with all the many
legged creatures under the floorboards peddling
hard past the places I have been before—
Sioux Lookout, Nakina, Armstrong, Thunder Bay,
beyond nowwhere the arctic summer ending—
In Northern Ont. colour fading on the few
red leaves left and winter's stencil ready,
creek racket muted to cold medley
over stones with ice tinkling:
along the roads in pickup trucks the hunters,
with moose and bear corpses,
their guts removed and frozen to shapes of death—
Across the road ahead a live moose lumbers, trying to
escape death, and the brown blunderbuss of fur climbs
a hill slowly beyond the red Ford passing—I hear his
heartbeat here in odd-numbered rhythm for every even-
numbered foot above the sea the mountain reaches to—

Sound: *Tone changes, becomes drowsy, hypnotic—*

I am asleep by the side of the road.
My voice sounds only
inside my head and I am wondering
where the moose and myself are going,
even the reason for going is not clear:
a red mark on my cheek of knuckles,
and holding the wheel hard,
the red Ford squirts down the road
near sunset and a vast crimson cummerbund
wrapped around earth's belly near Winnipeg—

4

Older voice:

The earth flattens
out and I am small and naked and lost,
reading the road map west—
And I know in my mind that all this is a poem,
which is to say the land the sky and myself,
interelation, reaction and rhythm,
drumming wheels and my own blood a part of it,
and the discovery that is not knowledge,
is the song of sun and rain on the windshield,
that is not an end in itself is not life,
life in itself the discovery
in a poem that is a mode of being—
The red Ford squirts down the road without
me, for I am asleep in myself riding
dust storms across the prairie in a box car
during the Hungry Thirties so tired
that wakefulness is a dream-state—
Brandon, Neepawa, Pile-o-bones Regina, Indian Head,
all the names,
I feed on them like a hungry dead man
seeking food in words and meaning inside place,
riding into the far places that remain distant
in spite of the red Ford or the jostling box cars
of my long ago footsteps:
passing over like a leather and iron ghost,
knocking at doors for handouts in strange towns,
chopping wood for meals and moving west,

Sound: *Train and auto mingled by turns*

Older voice:

that other self finally coming to realize that solitude
is the natural state of things,
and what being alive is all about,
exiled inside yourself—

Sound: *Wheels up, then fade down and out*

Music: *Brief*

Older voice:

Broadview where I was an hour younger
in the prairie time change
twenty years ago, and now regain that hour,
when railway cops deloused the train of bums,
all but me, the young louse, and another old guy,
a father to the world and the world was old—
We made it riding thru Broadview,
inside a threshing machine on a flatcar,
and all the others had to walk—

Sound: *Clanking of couplings as train moves out. Voices echo.*
          Fade down background for this episode

Younger self:

(HUMMING SOTTO VOCE)
Old Mother Goose, she lived in a shoe,
and walked it wherever she wanted to go—

Old hobo:

What are you mutterin about, kid?

Younger self:

(ORDINARY VOICE) (BUT A LITTLE EXCITED)
Nothin—just if the cops will look in here—

Old hobo:

They won't. (CALM) There's the highball. Listen!

Sound: *Train's toot-toot of departure*

Younger self:

What'll they do with us if we get caught?

Old hobo:

The universe'll explode and your mother will come—,
They'll lock me up and call the undertaker—

Younger self:

(DISGUSTED SOUND)

Old hobo:

(SERIOUS) I wanna tell you something, kid—

Younger self:

Well, it's kinda hard for me not to listen—

Old hobo:

Don't you get smart—

Younger self:

Go ahead and tell me, tell me—

Old hobo:

It's the way you board a moving box car—

Younger self:

(SNORTS)

Old hobo:

(PATIENTLY) Look! The iron ladder is at the front of
the car,
I seen you take the rear ladder twice since Brandon.
If you ever miss that ladder you're gone.

Younger self:

Gone? Gone where?

Old hobo:

Gone dead between cars, mashed under the wheels,
and the brakies sell what's left for dogfood.

Younger self:

(AFTER BRIEF PAUSE) Thanks.

Old hobo:

None needed. You get killed the rest of us don't get out
of jail till 1970 A.D.,
and I ain't got that much time—

PAUSE

Younger self:

You're really my friend, I can see that.
(SOTTO VOCE)
Old Mother Goose she lived in a train,
she fell underneath and died in the rain—

Music: *Brief*

Older self:

The red Ford squirts down the road,
past Piapot, Gull Lake, High River, Picture Butte,
Crowsfoot, Claresholm and Fort Whoopup,
dinosaur badlands and the Cypress Hills,
where amino acids that constituted life
in the great reptiles are dispersed and bleached
beneath the prairie sun,
their ghosts stride bellowing under potash
and grainfields awaiting the chance instant
of being riding eternity's carousel—
(VOICE CHANGES TONE AND INFLECTION)
The land changes here, in southern Alberta,
prairies ripple into hills like breasts of women,
coulees clawed out by spring runoffs,
and occasional jagged shoulders
hunching up out of bed rock,
but mostly smoothness, green undulations—
Piegan Indian country, rivers the Blackfoot crossed,
their descendants hitch hikers at the roadside,
war parties disarmed by the baby bonus,
their broncs hauling milkwagons,
their drums sound under the skin—
I hear them
inside my own skin-deep bone-hard tiredness
that loops me sideways like a yo-yo,

and I sleep by the side of the road—
(SLEEPING VOICE, SOFTER TIMBRE)
Of course the land is a woman,
a woman I know—
The smooth hills are a woman's breasts,
the wind your breathing from the near mountains,
the land slowly becoming flesh
under green lipstick, under pine perfume,
under the jig-saw landscapes of cities,
a woman I invented,
who might be real and probably isn't,
but corresponds to a real woman
in a conversation I also invented—
and say, I love you,
words that my dislike of makes necessary to say:
and she may reply:

Woman:

It's hard for me to say these things—

Older self:

Then I will write you a poem to say them—

Woman:

It's not because of poems that I—

Older self:

(HARSH) But the weather turned round,
black rain squirting on the windshield
of the red Ford racing down the road
among the shouldering foothills at seventy
miles an hour and she is gone—
I am almost awake under spruce and tamarack
among the high mountains—

Music: *Brief*

Sound: *Train*

Older self:

Red prowling lanterns in railway yards,
brakies and cops making their rounds,
signals blinking stop and go,
couplings crash in the still mountains,
a last highball silencing the crickets—
The huge engine sighs like a fat man,
seems to stumble and fall forward,
an old fat man growing younger—
And maybe a dozen men and boys
break cover from the trackside bushes,
racing alongside in the hobo Olympics,
vaulting into empty cars,
bumping breathless onto gondolas,
the jobless and homeless, farmers' sons
and factory labourers, womanless men,
climbing iron ladders into the night
(at the front ends of the box cars),
finding temporary peace in an iron racket,
the jarring hurry that shakes the world
to a violent blur that stops the heart—

Sound: *Motor car sounds fade background then hold down and out later*

Older self:

Climbing those same hills in a red Ford:
Coleman, Blairmore, Michel, Fernie,
dirty coal towns between green mountains,
and think of myself, the frightened boy,
riding on top of a red box car,
so high clouds are near neighbours,
suspended in a great blue cage,
where light comes up below—
(VOICE CONTAINS THE YOUNGER SELF IF POSSIBLE)
from tumbled valleys, green threads of rivers,
where mile-deep glaciers crawled once,
twice and three times in geologic ages,
white gravestones over the giant reptiles,
the first skittering mammals, the first human hunters
from across the Bering, fur-clad Asian tourists,
inching beneath shimmering walls of ice

as far south as the ice allowed
—along streams of raging meltwater;
lame old men left behind at hunger camps,
women dying of childbirth under skin tents,
and morning glittering its million diamond points
on the cloak of ice around them—
Finally, if they were lucky,
sighting the black specks like hairy landslides
moving far down the bright cul-de-sac,
trapped in a tangle of boulders,
surrounded like barnyard cattle,
thudding flint arrows pounding their life,
become red flesh at an out door butcher's,
the brute brain cold, the man-high tusks
trophies for hunters dancing around a fire—
(MUSING)
All of it nearly meaningless now,
except that the thing itself is meaning,
and those billion roving specks of life
under and over the earth,
reptile and mammal, hunters and food gatherers,
make a long chain stretching backward,
trace the features of a human animal,
vestigial tail and saltwater blood,
lungfish and dodo,
mapped on a boy's face riding the box cars west,
cinders beating back from trumpeting engine,
the journey from point A to point B,
starting point obscure the end oblivion,
which is not to lessen the journey itself,
the quality of of it, the exultance
in mountains and rivers—a woman's face
in my mind that escapes now,
leaps melting ice corridors,
beyond this stone platform in space,
to touch an absolute it can only imagine,
which is perhaps a crumb of stone,
a swirl of vapour a gaseous cloud,
changing into something else without witnesses—
The red Ford labours a little,
but the maker guarantees nothing,
eight cylinders pound in almost unison

11

Sound: *Car seems to be missing a little*

Older self:

for some listening celestial mechanic—
I stop at a mountain village for a sandwich,
eyeing bristly chin in restaurant mirror,
eyes two fried eggs on toasted cheeks—
Again driving I watch a hooting diesel
batter the canyon walls with sound,

Sound: *Diesel*

Older self:

and know these are my hangups:
I'm haunted by trains
riding down windistance in my mind,
snowflakes melting on black metal:
and rails run down the day's horizon,
a white eye slants on hogback hills,
thru midnight zero pullmans pass,
and spike their echoes to the trees—
In the long body of the land I saw your own,
the mountain peaks,
the night of stars,
the words I did not speak
and you did not,
that yet were spoken—
(ALTERED VOICE)
The myth includes Canada,
inside the brain's bone country;
my backyard is the Rocky Mountain trench
—wading all summer in glacier meltwater,
hunters with flint axes stumble south—
I take deed and title to ancient badlands
of Alberta around Red Deer:
and dinosaurs peer into Calgary office buildings—
Dead Beothucks of Newfoundland track down my blood;
Dorsets on the whale-coloured Beaufort Sea
carve my brain into small ivory fossils,
where all the pictures were,

that show what it was like to be alive
before the skin tents blew down—
The myth includes a woman,
a woman your love can't reach:
only the long slope of breast and thigh are hers,
her black eyes flashing are the continent's anger,
—my letters fall to silence at her land's white foot,
and waves have washed away her answer—
I gather together all the best things I am,
and all the worst—yours equally:
the scarlet maple leaves that brush your hand,
and mountains are my gifts beneath your feet—
Woman and country, both melt in one,
love ends with life, begins in what you are—
The red Ford squirts down mountain roads,
containing myself and is itself
contained by mountains and the brain's bone country,
the myth includes—

ORATORIO FOR SASQUATCH, MAN, AND TWO ANDROIDS

Margaret Atwood

Sasqua

I am th

maybe

Man:

His hou

he surr

Androi

I am pla

buttons

Androi

I too an

It ha

blur

films

for t

POEMS FOR VOICES

ERRATUM

Page 14, Oratorio For Sasquatch, Man, And Two Androids, by Margaret Atwood.

Delete the first eleven lines, beginning "I am the subject . . . ", and ending ". . . too long".

The CBC regrets any embarrassment caused the author by the inclusion of these lines in the broadcast and in this book.

Sasquat

Along the side of the mountain
the air is rippling; my trees
move back their branches, I can
hear the earth break under hard feet.

They are not animals, there are
three of them, I can smell them:
one of the old kind, smell of smoke and stone;
I have known him.

Two of the new kind: metal smell,
fear stink, like rotting fish; and the poison smell,
bright hot smell that burns when it hits you.

Why have they entered my place?
What are they asking?
The leaves are my ears,
they will listen for me.

Music: *(briefly)*

Man:

We will stop here
but we can make no fire;
fire offends him.
This is the border
of the silent region,
it is time to step over.
His house has no walls or ceiling:
it has only entrances,
it has only doors;
the doors are invisible.
He is waiting, he surrounds you.
Now you must tell me
who you are under
your sewn cloth surfaces, tell me
why you have come.

Android 2:

I am plated with flags, with badges;
my eyes are gold buttons,
around my head is a crown of pennies;
banners float from me, under my leather
jacket my skin
pimples itself with jewels
arranged in the shapes of medals,
growing and fading.

In front of me the forest is
alive, complicated, five-

dimensional; my hero
signals flash in its darkness, my feet
are knives, they cut level;

behind me the land stretches
flattened, laid with straight
squares.
            There are only
four directions. I blaze
paths, I untangle.

Man:

Here there are no maps,
here there are no trails;
the treetrunks you slashed
to show you the way back
have already healed themselves behind you.

Android 1:

It has been lurking
blurred near the edges of jerky
films, of damaged photographs
for too long; its deep footprints dissolve
in the rain as soon as they are
seen. It slides away
from us into caves of air, into burrows
made by treeshadows, takes refuge
in the eye's confusions.

I want it to be seen,
want it placed
among the mind's white
lists of things;
            it is my
past, it must be known,
it must be legible.

Man:

He cannot be read,
he can only be heard;
because he has no language

he speaks to each man in his own language.
The syllables are within you.
Once you have been to his land
you may enter and leave at will,
though few return from that journey
unchanged.
    The doors open always
here in this forest
under the ground, where the light is green
and the seasons and rivers flow backwards.

(background music)

Listen: now you can hear
the drone of the heavy sun as it travels
in its groove over the trees.
Look: at your feet a stone
has given birth to a smaller stone.
These are his words moving
where we may see them.

Android 1:

I see only fallen
leaves, I see only ferns,
I see only a repetition
of the morning's details;
birdsongs hit my ears
as random facts; twigs and
patches of open sky, water
seeping in moss, criss-
cross of slanting
logs, a lack of pattern.

Man:

That is because you have not yet learned
to use your true eyes.
Your eyes are locked,
your eyes are frozen:
you have used them too long as lenses.

You must discard these failed eyes,
these pieces of dead glass

that come between you and the world.
Let your hard sight melt:
then you will see as I do.

Android 2:

Tell us how to find it.
How do we recognize it?
Does it lie in wait?
Does it howl?
Does it leave signs, scratches
in soft earth? Does it walk in snow?
How do we recognize it?
Tell us how to find it.

Man:

I came to know him first
when I was young;
I wanted to learn wisdom.
He met me in a dream,
we struggled and I named him.
He ran towards me
and disappeared into my head.
Since then I have talked with him many times.
Some say he is an animal: he has fur
like an animal's, and sharp teeth;
others say he is a man, or something
that was once a man; his hands are a man's,
his eyes face forward.

To me he is neither;
what he is for you
will depend on what he wishes to show you,
what he is for you
will depend on what you want from him.

Android 1:

I want to drain the
shade cast by its furred
history across my clean
rubberskin body,
delete its growled hog

sounds, its rancid
armpit smell.

I want to explain
it; fit it
in; pin it; label
its separate parts, its habits;
with the small blades of my
fingers trace its outline.

I want to turn it to
plastic, to metal;
clear, functional
as I am.
I want to forget.

Android 2:

I have hunted in other jungles,
each one pushed me closer.
I have hunted other animals:
behind the brown mask
of the bear, the yellow
mask of the lion, the
horned mask of the deer,
I expected always to see it,
the beast no-one acknowledges,

the final mask: the animal
who is a man covered with fur.
It tracks me, it walks
at night over the lawn,
in through the neo-
colonial door, over
the walls of my room.

Soon I must kill the last fear,
nail it to the wall,
a neat hole marked on its forehead.

Man:

I have not understood.
I thought the guns were to shoot food.
I thought you wanted to learn from him
as I learn; now I see
you want to know, to control him
in your hands, pick him apart,
number and separate
his lungs, his arteries, his brain
so you can call the pieces
by your names, not by his own.

But you are wrong: he can never
be known: he can teach you only
about yourself.

I must go alone to ask his forgiveness
for having brought you; and to ask him
what must be done with you.

Do not be afraid; stay here.
I will return with his answer.
Perhaps he will give you your wish.
Who can tell? He cannot be predicted.
Perhaps he will allow you to kill him:
even he is not immortal.
He has strange ways of teaching.

Music:

Android 1:

My days are stainless
steel arranged in rows,
my nights are sheets
pulled up over the face

I am lined with tiles,
I move inside
a glass capsule; my hands and
feet, reaching, sense only
cool, smooth, clear.

I am dust—
free. I am sealed

Android 2:
I note the hawk
turning there in the sky
on his tall wind column.
The eye measures, draws
an X on him;
the eye tenses, stretches, is
a tentacle, a hot whistle,
the eye is a bullet, expands
to a red wound

It brings him down,
claws gripping
nothing, wings with the air
knocked out from under;

I have won
again.

Android 1: *(rapidly) (in almost a prose voice)*
My aim is knowledge,
to know a thing I must probe it.

First I will capture it
with nets traps helicopters dogs pieces
of string holes dug in the ground doped food
tranquilizer guns buckshot thrown stones
bows and arrows

Then I will name the species
after myself

Then I will examine it
with pins tweezers flashlights microscopes telescopes
envelopes statistics elastics
scalpels scissors razors lasers cleavers axes
rotary saws incisors osterizers pulverizers and fertilizers.

I will publish the results
in learned journals.

Then I will place a specimen
in each of the principle zoos
and a stuffed skin
in each of the principle museums
of the western world.

When the breed nears extinction due to
hunters trappers loggers miners farmers
directors collectors inspectors

I will set aside a preserve consisting of:
       1 mountain
       1 lake
       1 river
       1 tree
       1 flower
       1 rock
and 1 tall electric fence.

Android 2:

The things I want from it are:
1) power
2) fame
3) money

I will get these things
pardon me, achieve these goals
by:

1) shooting it, thus proving it can be killed
   but only by one with skill and courage
   such as myself
2) posing for a front-page picture and/or a
   TV documentary with my boot on its neck and
   one hand casually on my hip
3) exhibiting, for a fee, the remains
   which will have been preserved by:
   a) stuffing
   b) formaldehyde
   c) freezing in ice

I will then make replicas from
—fur coats
—leather gloves
—putty
—inner tubes
—piano keys
—modelling clay
—human hair

I will open a nationwide chain of man-monsters
I will retire at forty
and go fishing

I will have a recurring dream:
one day when I am standing in a shallow
pool casting for trout
a hand will reach out and pull me under.

Android 1:

What have you been saying?
I have been thinking.
Have you been saying anything?
How long have we been waiting?
(pause)
The birds seem to have stopped. No squirrels.
Only trees. No wind
in the branches either.
              Look, the sun
is getting brighter
edges of moss
glitter   clear orange
mushrooms leap
up from the dead leaves
              far above there, purple
and blue swoops, drops
in a huge rain

behind my eyelids light
moves in a web of
pain   such fine
focus   look

there, look
          at the stem
of the sapling: a glass
filled slowly with green water

Android 2:

I can't hear you
I can see your mouth
moving, but I can't hear you
Listen: inside
          a sound
my head is stretched out
long and hollow   corridor
the treetrunks echo each other

Android 1:

the stones are
               breathing
                         soft
               their pores open

Android 2:

vibration
          like dynamite, a boulder
exploded miles away

thick wool footsteps
                         the air
lifting and setting down

the branches roar

the leaves are attacking
my ears

Music: *Cue*

Sasquatch:

You have searched for me, questioned
my mountains, dug for my
bones among landslides
brandished the rumours
of me in your cities

24

collected my footprints
patiently through the years,
yet you have never found me.
You have been ruthless in
my valleys, you have invaded
my sleep
         you run in my dreams,
small hairless enemies, gleaming and
weaponed, inquisitive,
barbed with instruments, addicted
always to death

Now you have evoked me,
now you will see me clearly.
Hunters, you are my nightmare,
as I am yours.

Music
(crescendo)

Android 1:

My eyes hurt. What
was it? What did we hit?

Android 2:

It was a thing like a grizzly bear
walking on its hind legs;
I saw its teeth, it had
pig's eyes, tiny and brute
with the thought of slaughter

Android 1:

It was
a giant man, his eyes thundered, his hair
was standing up all over his head
like red fire; his fingers were
sharp claws; but he was smiling,
he was looking through my face and smiling,
he lifted one hand . . . .

Man:

There was no animal,
there was no man with claws.
It was my body you shot at.

When I had spoken with him
I turned back to find you;
I heard his owl's voice calling my name;
it was noon; I knew then I would die.

At the edge of the clearing
I paused; you were sitting down;
by your eyes I could tell
that he was near.

Suddenly he came upon me,
the crash of a tree falling;
for an instant I felt his strength, his power
within me; the god
and I were one;
through me he was speaking to you.

Android 2:

It was a bear

Android 1:

It was
a giant man, his hair
was flames

Man:

You were not used to seeing.
You could see only through your fear
which blurs vision.

But the god has not denied you.
It is you who have denied the god.

He would have given you knowledge of life,
you chose instead the knowledge
of death. He has shown you what you are.

He has gone out of my body,
he leaves me here for you,
a husk, a trophy,
an animal skin,
a memory to take back with you
from the dark forest
to your lighted cities.

Now you have killed the god;
you have what you wanted.

Music: *Cue*

Sasquatch:
A wound has been made in me,
a hole opens in my green flesh;
I see that I can be broken.

Two are moving away,
the third remains.

Come, my brother,
your blood runs into the earth,
at last I can hear you clearly;

you are telling me
that those who have destroyed you
will return in other bodies
to destroy me also;
already their saws, their axes
hack at my borders;
to murder my pines, my cedars
is to murder me.

Their straight roads diminish
my space, my kingdom.

We will go to the other country.
Under the mountains there is a sea,

it is summer here, there
it is winter. We will sit

together by that frozen shore

until the killers have been changed
to roots, to birds

until the killers have become
the guardians and have learned
our language

waiting to be delivered,
waiting to be made whole.

Music
(optional)

The End

ΠOTEƒ FROM AΠD AMOΠO THE WARƒ

John Newlove

1 Your drink is twice as strong as mine is.
   Your mouth is twice as fair as mine is.
   Your hair is sweeter than mine is.
   You smile where I could wish to smile.
   You sleep when I could wish to sleep.

   I wish to dream on the page, it is so white,
   through our centuries of blood.

2 Were the bunks neat in Auschwitz?
   Was the soul's blonde efficiency repulsed
   by the messy blankets of Jews and Gypsies?—If
   they had blankets, those who surrendered
   immortal teeth of gold, surrendered rings, piles
   of prosthetics tabulated in the avenues
   between the wooden huts, and all else?

3 Dead arrogant kings
       bearded in gold,
   beautiful to archaeologists,
   living on slaves, slaves—
       my people,
   having come out of Asia,
   your sons the seven Osmanli mutes,
       who strangle and smile,
   what have you done
   but bow and wait
   for the petty lords of creation,

heirs of the floods and the plagues
    and dead with gold
a crust on the rotted faces,
    till you after some centuries or so
    could use a new plow to conquer Europe?

4   State trumpets blown, flutes lipped,
    clarinets soprano wavering. . . .

                  they resume the past
    from which they are trying to escape—

5   In the end you don't even know yourself,
    only the hill you must climb; but not even
    the hill: a bump on it, one hump of grass,
    a flint, a blade thin in the wind as you climb,
    each step, each breath, taken in a dissimilar time—

6   What is the reward of faith?
    new horizons?
        new lies, then a glamor
    that retreats from truth
    as it advances?—

7   And how, after each little separation,
    we seem to have to learn again
    to know each other, as awkward strangers do—
    the slightest kiss, our accidental hands, our eyes
    that waver off each other, as if we had not been
    nakedly in love. . . .

8   I would like to whistle softly in your ear
    to recall to you a tune we might have played,
    if I could remember it. Instead I sit reading
    of man's perpetual wars,
    of how he says he strides toward the stars—

9   Not only blood, there were the factories,
    the manufacturers of eunuchs
    in Verdun and Sicily—

10   Move slightly, man born to die;
no sense how long the time
or short. In accidents or the inevitable
end of age, single or double,
spirit or flesh, you cease to be—

11   Among the wars
the poet walks along
in his mind,
from the start
gone wrong,
unable to find
some simple part

that he might make
into a simple song
or phrase to take
as medicine
when he walks along
in his mind,

when his mind soars,
from the start
gone wrong—

12   And to see men
attempting to do things,
and their women,
wary, protecting them,
wolves, distrusting
all strangers, smiling
like guards—

13   Twinned figures slowly pace round.
Now a circle is so small, so tight each stares
into the other's face. Over the bones
the skin tightens; white shadows lengthen in the eyes;
the hair, pulled down and knotted, black, crusted with blood,
covers the ears; thorns pierce the lips. A sick dog whines

and licks the stiff draining sores that cover it.
A clock ticks. A clock ticks. Muscles twitch.

This is night. Odd bruises sit in beds of bloody fat.
Underneath the lids the eyes jerk back and forth,
watching the figures pace slowly. Left in the dreaming mind
there is no sound but that of an ignorant dying animal
given to sacrifice, sure of nothing but its death—

14   They carry their heads beautifully,
      but what they carry is trash—

15   As among the wars
      and the fears
      we sail
            or kill—
      wanderers. . . .

16   —And what one would have thought
      to have brought forward
      to build on
               has become one's life,
      with no additions.

17   Black noise—

18   There's a man inside there, dying,
      as you in your homogalactic excitement watch
      the fuming awkward plane
      fifty-five funny years ago
      dive in twisty smoke
      into a poison sea of shell-ploughed earth:
      it is a movie.
              For you it would be much more bitter
      just to walk in the streets
      than to watch those older deaths again.

19   The blue trees grow from year to year
      and seem to have no thoughts,
      though I have heard it said
      they scream when we kill before them—

20   Today, when the sun does not rise;
      today when the government cannot stop the snow;
      today, as the murders cross the television screen;
      today as the headlines are hopelessly accepted;
      today, while watching a real-life neo-gothic fistfight;
      today while on the outskirts of no novelist;
      today, during the shakiness of human life;
      today during our constant killing ignorance,
      declaring our deaths by a continuous rehearsal of them,
      we live and try to love—
                        ourselves, at least,
      if no others—

21   Orator, when you see your similarly-shirted audience
      heave upon its hams and wait for an excuse
      to rise, to stomp, remember—
      they want to listen to your visible screams,
      they'll want to break your own bones
      if they cannot break the bones you want broken:
      either you must be roaring on the podium
      or dying in the trashy streets.
      The audience does not want to listen to your dreams,
      but to its own.

22   —And give us a little pity too
      for the last drink in the whisky bottle
      Sunday afternoon, for the calcium in our spines,
      for the daily prejudiced paper, the constant liars,
      the people who think war is a high-school debate,
      the ones who take freedom away
      and then return all but a portion,
      congratulating themselves on their generosity
      and their care for others, as gradually
      our portions get smaller—

23 —Save us from sociologists who, if they are accurate,
    have not the slightest sense of humor—

24 —Forgive us for whom civilization consists of acquiring
    the correct mental addictions, those of us who act
    as if we hated the human in ourselves, knowing
    there is enough to hate in the human in ourselves—

25 The wars, the slaveries, no dead men redeemed by poems,
    no humiliations redressed with songs, no chain scars
    in the soul erased with apologies
    a hundred years late—it was all a mistake. . . .
    the simple everyday savagery of parent to child
    or child to parent, brother to brother, sister to sister—

26 —The torture goes on forever as we in perpetual motion
    breed and destroy ourselves for any reason we can think of,
    even intelligent ones. . . .

27 —All of which we have always known,
    in despair and amusement at ourselves
    as we continue to dirty and ruin
    everything we touch. . . .

28 Everything we touch. Especially,
    forgive those of us who must say:
    Only my accidents are graceful. . . .

29 Well, a certain fame is got by burning temples
    as well as by building them, and in the end
    the things are famous, loved, not their makers
    particularly. Gods can inhabit
    the meanest structures while
    fabulous piles are empty of anything but fools.

30   And there is an egypt of the mind,
grotesque, mysterious, sacrificial,
where the dunes are piling and unpiling
their arabesques, coiling about some point
not grasped, some secret living to be learned,
desperately longed for. . . .

31   Blue and green commingling, the muscley sea
sliding through the mind, a notion of deeper rivers
than those that run over the earth; among the stars,
currents in the bright mixture pulsing, something
that might be there to save us, as it seems
we cannot save ourselves or do not want to—

32   To be willingless. To be willing. . . .

33   Willingless and willing, as when
the pickup truck went around
a slight curve to the right,
years ago, and stopped. Off the road,
a small triangular piece of level ground,
a wooden shack, a quick shallow river,
and beyond the trees again as far as could be seen,
night coming, thoughts of bears, the sound
of crisp leaves rattling as bits of wind
brushed off them, a place unknown and feared
and the driver saying: This
is as far as I go, and leaving me alone
with the cold and the coming dark
and with my own ignorance and cowardice
to endure as best I could—in odd places
the shine of snow still protected by bushes
and clumps of thin grass, packrats
waiting in the shack. . . .

34   But what should we expect of our memories,
except remembrance? We are so adept,

so practised in false hopes, so able to read
the slightest changes in a face,
the slightest intonations in a voice,
as indications of things
that do not exist, affirmations
never considered by the other. . . . only when our hopes
disappear do we see the truth we wished so fervently
to forget—it is so hard to think of anyone
except ourselves; a life is only made of moments,
sad as they are, whether they are shared or not—

35   We spend our time waiting for letters
that have never been written:
Dear J., I love you,
why don't you come to me. Come into me.
Dear J., You've won a hundred thousand dollars.
Dear J., I like your poem. I like you.
Dear J., I love you, I like you, you're fine,
you've won a toby mug of Haile Selassie.

How fine to be lonely, to be neglected,
always to have that to complain of—
the unringing telephone—rather than a bellyache
or a sore back. How odd that mental hypochondria
produces poetry and technology
though pain brings only self-loathing and false pity.

Mementoes: thefts from futures
we will not allow ourselves to have;
and, knowing we are nothing,
we must invent—stirrups, staples, holy days
and gods to fit them. We wish
there were more answers than questions,
but there are not. Why is the sky blue, daddy,
said the son of Peking man, the cannibal.

36   Elsewhere, two empires existed in the air of time,
both warring and working, both magical,
encapsuled and bloody, building,
tilling, reaping, raiding, raping, toiling
with heaped masonry, paving roads,

carving palaces, creating statues
of the eagle and the jaguar gods; while they did,
ships sailed the oceans in search of gold,
land, slaves, war, what was called honor,
religion. A third empire had crumbled
though the cities stood, abandoned
in the vicious green jungle; survivors
haunted the cult sites and the stone calendars:
and farmers will still sow new seed
though the masters change. In one empire
the priests danced in the skins of their victims,
the great drums boomed, happy sacrifices
climbed long stone stairs to death against the sky
as whistles blew. The daggers descended
to appease the invented gods again, the empire
was upheld again, rain came again.

In the other empire the gods of the sun
sat living on their ornamented stools;
roads extended to the borders of knowledge
and avarice, populations were exchanged, conquered tribes
learned new languages, the regiments of civilization
marched farther along the cultivated coast
and into the mountains. What must be done is done.

The empire of blood and the empire of sun
were sweating gold, sweating silver, sweating war,
the empire dead in the jungle tried to reassemble,
while from another world in search of honor
and profit ships sailed the unknown seas,
drifting through green water to the ignorant world
where the welcoming victims, in wishfulness
and confusion, would wait to receive new gods
and different virtues, different crimes.

37 Deaths, deaths. . . . and driving alone at night
through our deserted beautiful country
in which only the trees seem alive—

38 —Waking up mornings,
      my mouth full of blood—

39 —It seeming to be such a difficult life,
      and yet so easy for it not to be that way—

40 What breasts
      shall I press against,
      whose hair breathe?

41 —As water rings in the musical hillside sewers
      in a false spring—

42 —hoarding regrets, and leaving one loved
      like putting on a new disease each time—

43 —And the ghost that sings in my blood
      a mortal, everything waiting
      for its boat-shaped grave, receiver
      of the dead, ender of the sad tricks
      we play on ourselves, ender of foolish lives
      and foolish loves greatly desired, ending
      of the moaning instruments of lives
      that repeat and repeat themselves, happily
      sorrowful, in sorrow happily repeating
      the past from which they are trying to rise—

44 You smile where I could wish to smile,
      you sleep when I could wish to sleep.
      It is not the milk-bearing tree I dream of,
      but the one that seeps blood, or trees
      exploding like firecrackers in the winter's cold.

45 —Caught in the maze of life
      and knowing only that we end—

46   Avoiding the horror of infinity—

47   —With questions:
     Was I a lover you had
     out of your kindliness
     in wintertime?—

48   —Is today the day I got old?—

49   —Knowing you die, what would you do
     if you could change and change
     until you died?—

50   If you were in the air,
     would you be a bird?

     If you were able, would you wish to be?
     If you were able, would you sing?

     If you cared to be, thinking
     of what life is, no revenge,

     would you want to fly?—knowing
     below, and as you fly, in the green concealed pit
     the hunter with his sighted shotgun lies?

DOCTOR UMLAUT'S EARTHLY KINGDOM

Phyllis Gotlieb

Baritone:
Good evening

Soprano:
good evening

Tenor:
good evening

Alto:
hullo

All:
if you want to know who we are we're a
bunch of worn-out carnies putting up a crummy
carnival in a vacant lot

Undertaker (tenor):
I'm a former seller of potato-peelers and
ex-vendor of eggbeaters
who fell into the undertaking business
because that's where the money is

Girl (soprano):
I'm an innocent country lass
who was betrayed

Whore (alto):
I'm a whore with a heart of brass

Clockseller (tenor):
I'm-a-highly-nervous-and-unstable-seller-of

clocks-and-watches-and-I-don't-think-I'll-be
able-to-stop-talking-till-I-die

Missus Brown (soprano, a bit over-ripe and sly):
I'm Missus Brown, dear

Alto:
what are we waiting for?

Tenor:
the man coming
down the street

Soprano:
down the twilight street

Tenor:
the magisterial man
with the top hat frock coat snakehead cane
and everything that goes with that

Alto:
spade beard striped pants grey spats
and he's carrying
a black case

All:
good evening

Umlaut (baritone)
good evening

Ladies and gentlemen I address you here at the busy
crossroads of life
                I watch your cheerful faces and
listen to your happy laughter as you pass in the
street
     and I know what misery pain sorrow heartache
and grief those smiles cover that laughter drowns those
cheerful voices conceal
                  and
to ease those aches those pains those griefs

I am bringing you

release!
for I am Doctor Umlaut! Doctor Umlaut!
and I bring you Doctor Umlaut's
King of Pain!

Doctor Umlaut's Panacea
Panchreston and Pharmacopeia!

wherever it gets you you rub it on
one touch of heaven and the pain is gone

Onlooker (tenor):
but I ain't feelin no pain

Umlaut:
then wait for the rain!
everybody hurts in this vale of sorrow
if you don't get it today it'll get you tomorrow

in this pure glass bottle
no cheap plastic
price one dollar
plus five cents tax
and I'll tell you what it does:

Onlooker 2 (alto):
Doctor, will it cure my sacroiliac?

Umlaut:
rub it in!
if not you get your money back
if you hurry to catch me, I'm a busy man
and I've got to make a dollar wherever I can

Onlooker 3 (soprano):
will it cure a sliver?

Umlaut:
rub it in!
crisis, phthisis, fever, liver

catalepsy, narcolepsy, lycanthropy
ringworm, tapeworm, hookworm, bookworm
follicle mites
everything that bites!

Onlooker 1:
will it cure my hog?

Umlaut:
rub it in!
it'll cure your hog and your sheep and your dog
springhalt, windgalls, cracked teats
ringbone, garget, spavins and grease
sweeney, fistula, foundered feet
rub it in! rub it in! rub it in!

if you're stained with sin
rub it in!

if you're plagued with doubt
wipe it out!

if your heart is broken
glue it together
paint it on the sky and change the weather

Disturbers (tenor, alto):
yeah, yeah, blah, blah!
ah, rub it out, Umlaut
Umlaut!

Disturbers (tenor, alto, soprano):
if you're thirty-six years old and still wet the bed
can't make it with the girls, got a hole in your head
want your grandma brought back from the dead
ask Umlaut, Umlaut—out! out!

(not quite in unison)

go back where you came from, Umlaut
we don't want you here
Umlauts belong with circumflexes

Disturber 1 (alto):
nah, they're kin to the asterixes

Disturber 2 (tenor):
commas

Disturber 3 (soprano):
colons

Disturber 2:
codicils

Disturber 1:
you mean colophons, moron!

All three:
ah, go back home to the ampersands
Umlaut!

Umlaut:
Umlaut, I'm Umlaut
lout, I'm Umlaut!

fools, don't laugh
don't sneer

heed the words of the prophet and seer!

for he has decreed
and he has declared

that the laughter of fools
is as the crackling of thorns
beneath the cauldrons of hell
wherein the demons dwell

when the doors are darkened
and the evening cools
when the sound of the grinders
whispers down the street

they're whetting their pitchforks
and sharpening their horns

for the laughter of thorns
is as the crackling of fools!

but if you're so sure that you're absolutely pure
as the snow that falls before the morning light
then go away
who wants you to stay?
an ounce of prevention's worth a pound of cure

and I'll tell *you*
what you can do?

if you don't want to sin eat Christie's crackers they're
                                        sealed in
if you don't want to crack use Polyfilla it caulks back
if you don't want to fall nail your skin to the wall
if you don't want to crawl give Avis a call
if you don't want to crack
if you don't want to fall
if you don't want to sin

but if you belong to the human race
got eyes ears nose and a mouth in your face
if you turn and turn and never find a place
freeze in the sun and burn in the rain

then you need Doctor Umlaut's King of Pain!

Undertaker (tenor):
here's Missus Brown, here's Missus Brown
a goldtooth diadem planted in her crown
and her net bag and her buckled shoes
hatpin and zircon

Missus Brown (soprano, *can sing if she finds a tune to fit***)**
I'll be lying in the ground with my gold teeth
I'll be lying in the ground with my treasure buried round
when I'm rotting in the grave
then they'll say: now she'll behave
I'll be lying in the ground with my old gold teeth

Undertaker:
hey Missus Brown, hey Missus Brown
is your old man Bluey here in town?

Missus Brown:
nah, love, he's doin a stretch

Umlaut:
Madam, Madam, the King of Pain is here to serve you

Missus Brown:
gimme a bottle, sweetie, I'll
rub it on my foundered feet

Alto *(distantly)*:
come ride the

Tenor *(distantly)*:
come ride the
merrygoround

Missus Brown:
quite a carnival
you're runnin here

Alto *(still far away)*
ferris wheel

Tenor *(likewise)*
carousel

Umlaut:
one night only, Madam
perhaps you'll want two

Missus Brown:
one for each foot, dearie?
what do you think you can do me for?

Undertaker:
hey Missus, hey Missus Brown
don't you think it's time you thought of death?

Missus Brown:
sure love, to be sure love
I think of death each time I take a breath
what're you sellin now?
what've you got?
when it was potato-peelers
they got rusty
when it was eggbeaters
my cake sank
are you tryin to sell me
an annuity
in case my old man Bluey gets shot?
well he's only a common thief, dear
and he's so damn common he never brought in
a penny to spare
why can't us poor women have a Thief Relief?
it isn't hardly fair

Undertaker:
Missus Brown my love
it's you I'm thinking of
I'm selling caskets

Missus Brown:
hah

Undertaker:
complete with plot

Missus Brown:
hoo

Undertaker:
just behave, missus
and you'll save, missus
put a dollar in the pot

Missus Brown:
a dollar down and nowhere to go

Undertaker:
and once you die
you'll rise on high
swing with the angels
up in the sky

Missus Brown:
I'm lying in the ground with my gold teeth

Undertaker:
and be the envy
of the Ladies Auxiliary

I'll undertake to undertake to take you under sweetly
I'll send you under six feet down both neatly and completely
while the twenty-third psalm
keeps the mourners calm
with a min-i-mum of pain
I'll write a guarantee
in a hand so free
that you'll never come up again

Missus Brown:
ah, you're gonna preserve me
like old King Tut

Undertaker
alas, an undertaker's lot
is definitely not
an utterly happy one
no matter how he tries to stop the rot
it's a thing that can't be done
a mahogany box and a copper case give you only style and dash
and I've got to admit
he's doing it
for a max-i-mum of cash

Missus Brown:
what happens to the undertaker
when he dies?

Undertaker:
        he's taken over
by another undertaker
who shunts him down below the clover

Missus Brown:
I see! I see!
you don't have to tell me more
it ain't me you're waitin for, babe
it ain't me you're waitin for

The Company *(singing)*
what shall we do with your body, missus
where shall we hide your corpus, missus
where shall we heave your carcase, missus
ear-ly in the morning?

Missus Brown *(singing)*
heat it and serve it on paper dishes
carve it up into bait for fishes
yes, carve it into bait for fishes
ear-ly in the morning

Undertaker:
nah, that wouldn't be proper, lady
that sure wouldn't be proper, lady
somebody'd think it was awful shady
ear-ly in the morning

Missus Brown *(singing)*
drop it in the well and make three wishes
drop it in the well and make three wishes
just be sure you don't act suspicious
ear-ly in the morning

Umlaut:
please! that would cause pollution, Madam
horrifying pollution, Madam
hardly the best solution, Madam
ear-ly in the morning

Missus Brown *(singing)*
chop it up into fertilizer
that way no-one will be the wiser
chop it up into fertilizer
ear-ly in the morning

The Company *(singing)*
heave ho and up she rises
into the flowers and leaves she rises
maple and oak and pine she rises
into God's green morning!

Undertaker:
goodbye, so long Missus Brown
hope your old man Bluey's out soon

Missus Brown:
no hurry, love, there ain't no hurry
I'll be lying in the ground
with my treasure buried round
I'll be lying. . .
(Missus Brown fades out)

Umlaut:
that's one you didn't get
that's one you lost, my boy

Undertaker:
my trade may flourish like the green bay tree
but it's no joy to wash the dead
don't jeer at me
I never said
it was a joke or joy
in my house flowers never live
or children grow
death's angel is my cousin but I never said
he was my favourite relative

and I'll get her yet
her kind always wants to die respectable

Soprano *(far away)*
merrygoround, carousel

Alto *(faintly)*
fishpond and ferriswheel

Umlaut:
the race is not to Swift's no matter how
they pull the bull by the horn or slice the cow
for the fish in the net and the bird in the snare
can smother in the water and choke in the air
NOT A THROUGH STREET/NO THOROUGHFARE

but you can push back Death
shake your fist in his face
catch an extra breath
stay abreast of the race
get value for every second you gain
with Doctor Umlaut's King of Pain!

(distant voices of barkers:)

Alto:
try your luck, a quarter

Soprano:
try your skill, a quarter

Tenor:
take a shot, a quarter

Alto:
shoot to kill, thirty-five cents

Umlaut:
soldier, here's a bargain for you
soldier, got a minute or two
soldier?

Soldier *(the soldier's part is always taken by the two male
voices speaking in unison except where indicated)*
clear glass bottle?

Umlaut:
yes!

Soldier:
no cheap plastic?

Umlaut:
yes!

Soldier:
price one dollar
plus five cents tax?

Umlaut:
yes, yes!

Soldier:
why not? I've drunk everything else

Undertaker:
soldier, you want a nice cheap
convenient resting place
a real bargain?

Soldier:
there'll always be a place for me to die, man
and somebody to build a tomb for me where I'm not

Girl *(this part is spoken by the two women in unison)*
soldier

Soldier:
yes

Girl:
got a minute?

Soldier:
yes

Girl:
planning to do anything in it?

Soldier:
got a suggestion?

Girl:
yes! soldier, will you come to me come
with your musket fife and drum da-da-dum

Soldier:
I've been I've been wherever there is to be

Girl:
and you've seen whatever there is to see?

Soldier:
right left right:

I've shaken a spear with Caesar
shoved the elephants over the Alps
been shot in the eye with a crossbow
nailed to a crucifix (two sticks)

strung from a yardarm
hung from a tree

Girl:
for what? for what?

Soldier:
for raping and stealing and various other
kinds of larceny
had my skull split with a pike
stuck one or two heads on a spike
been split up the belly and watched my tripes
sliding like hot blue snakes

Girl:
it takes a lot of guts to be a soldier

Soldier:
say it again you can say it again with the
mud and the blood you can say it again

I've fought with a Maxim and a Martini
fought with a Bofors and a Bren
fought with an axe and an assegai
everything went and so did I
when I was called

most of the time

>   (*here the voices break step and the baritone
>   comes in with* "when" *as the tenor says* "good")

Tenor:
when it went (good
Baritone:
>   (when it went good

>   (*both*)

>   when I felt good
I went for the whores like a soldier should

and when I felt wild I might feed a child
or cradle the head of a wounded man

and I hold on to life as hard as I can

Girl:
if you want life, soldier
come on, come on
take it while there's time

Whore (alto)
ten and three

Umlaut:
who's this, who's she?

Whore:
ten and three

Undertaker:
coming down the midway

Whore:
my time is free

Undertaker:
down the oldest way in the world
in a dress with sleeves
feathered at the edge
with a purposeful walk in a purple dress with

Whore:
ten and three

Undertaker:
sleeves feathered at the edge
hey miss, hey miss, have you time for me?

Whore:
you? go on home to your wife

Umlaut:
are you interested in a balm to sustain you
throughout the ills and the evils that pain you?

Whore *(ultra-Brecht)*
I ain't buyin. I'm sellin.
I'm ten and three
I'm ten and three
at ten and three my time is free

three for the pillow and ten for the spread
and none for the shadow that falls on the bed

got your money? got your money?
put your money where your mouth is
never mind
old Vice Squad flat in the feet flat in the head
is giving me the eye: beg pardon sir
oh beg pardon sir, do you have the time?
yes miss oh yes miss it's ten-seventeen
a-young-miss-like-you shouldn't be out-in-a-place-like-this
oh thank you sir thank you sir I'm-going-home-right-now
yes sir thank you sir go spit in your mother's beer

as a girl who was fair I was called
by the young who were hairy the old who were bald
they made me their toy
and I gave them all joy
and a dose of the syph to each sweet mother's boy

now I'm old and tough
and my life's been rough
and if I was smart I'd say that was enough

but I walk my beat
in the hollow street
my shoes are too tight and I'm scared of the night
but my time is free
at ten and three
my time is free
my time is free

Broom-girl (soprano, *coming in from a distance***)**
who'll buy my brooms?

Whore *(growing fainter)*
my time is free

Broom-girl:
who'll buy my brooms?

Whore *(fading)*
ten and three

Broom-girl:
tenpenny brooms
pigeon-wing feather-dusters
my brooms are not ragged
but well-cut and round

Undertaker:
cherry-ripe, too, miss?
your lips are like cherries

Broom-girl:
my tenpenny brooms
are very well bound

Undertaker:
if you were selling branches of cherries, I'd buy them

Broom-girl:
buy my brooms
to sweep your rooms
chopcherry chopcherry jigajig

Umlaut:
miss, sweet miss, you seem to be ailing
your cheek is so pale and your eyes are so brimming
you seem to be
a lass with a lackaday

Broom-girl *(sweet but crisp)*
what can I say?
what else can I say?
it's the usual story I tell
how I loved him not wisely but too bloody well
he filled up my belly
and left me for Nelly
and I hope it's God truth that I'll meet him in hell

Undertaker:
what, in hell?

Broom-girl:
yes, in hell

Umlaut:
surely not in hell

Broom-girl:
hot crackling cinder-black and shrivelling
I've got brooms to sell and I'll see you in hell
John, for your
chopcherry chopcherry jigajig

Undertaker:
miss, I pity him

Broom-girl:
buy my brooms, pity me
(gently now)
did you show me pity, John,
never, John, no

will you lie with me on the bed
against my body rest your head
to feel the baby move within
and swear such love could be no sin?

no John, oh no, John
oh no, John, no, John, no

in that cold room so crabbed and mean
no broom will ever sweep it clean
I lie and sweat and curse the time
I must go clothed in blood and slime
in that place where the basins freeze
to scream the child between my knees
will you be there, to touch my hair
to kiss my bitten lips and swear
this is the crown of love? not you, John
never, John, not you

that's liniment you're selling, isn't it?
will that rub away a five-month belly?

Umlaut:
liniment has its limits

Undertaker:
so sweet a girl, so fresh and creamy

Broom-girl:
yes, I'd look good in one of your coffins, wouldn't I?
threepenny feather-dusters, who'll buy, who'll buy?

Whore *(faintly)*
I'm ten and three

Broom-girl *(fading)*
tenpenny brooms, tenpenny brooms

Whore *(very faint)*
my time is free

Clockseller (tenor)
who said time?
who said time?
who said time?
did I hear time?

Umlaut:
I believe something of the sort was mentioned

Undertaker:
go away, I'm tired of everything tonight

Umlaut:
the ladies are snubbing him

Undertaker:
everybody's selling
nobody's buying
business is a corpse
and I can't even bury it

Umlaut:
then you need Doctor Umlaut's King of Pain!

Clockseller:
and you need time time time and again gain gain
what I'm selling you is Time!

Undertaker:
another salesman

Clockseller:
I sell Time
in time pieces
in mortgages deeds rents and leases
in sundials sandglasses
candles and clepsydras
I sell mean time moon time

star time noon time
pendulums stopwatches
Nuremberg eggs!

and my time's
going cheap going cheap
and I get it get it get it
at the source:

there's a little old Timetaker in Geneva
in a cellar with a trapdoor and a deep steep step
and with his ratchets and his sprockets
and his springes and his springs
he begs borrows steals and bargains pieces of time
with demons, with angels, with popes and with kings
he catches tick in ratchets tock
in sprockets tick and springs tock
those demons tick those angels tock those popes
and those kings

and
he
brings
them
to
me!

and I pay for them

I pay for them
with my heart's drip blood drop
bright red heart's blood
heart's tick blood tock

and
I
bring
them
to
you!

there's a Rollex Westclox Timex to wear when you love
there's an Accutron Omega Waltham to wear when you die
and when you get to the Pearly Gate
you can tell Saint Peter he's running late
the race is won under the sun under the sky!

I sell Time Time Time I sell Time on the line
and the Alpha and Omega shall be mine mine mine!

Umlaut:
time, gentlemen, time
time to go
time to pack up the show

Clockseller:
sometimes time comes too close to me
talk to me, talk to me
say it isn't so
my heartclock mocks me
and my breath goes where the winds go
don't make me go

Alto:
the dawn is coming

Soprano:
cockadoodle, cockadoodle-doo

Clockseller:
cuckoo!

Alto:
cocorico, cucaricaru

Clockseller:
don't make me go

The Company:
the dawn is coming on its big fat feet
pick up, pick up, pick up your step
ditchdigger, steelwalker, time study man

don't tread on a crack
stiffen your back
hold up your head

The Men:
limber your hands
pull down the stands

Missus Brown:
cheer up, love, you'll soon be dead

The Women:
morning is coming with the voice of the bird
the sound of the grinders, the crackling of thorns
the nightwinds falter, the sun
straddles squares on the hopscotch street

The Company:
pick up, pick up, pick up your feet
hold up your head

Old Woman (alto):
I'm pickin up I'm pickin up
what's left over
bottles bag and old rags
I can't lift up my head because my back's crooked
my feet's a bunch of bones with corns on 'em
and I'm damned if I care about morning or night

here's a glove to put with one I found last year
they don't make a pair but they make two
left or right?

Umlaut:
Madam, I have a bargain for you
Madam, Madam, a bargain for you
here's my last bottle and it's going cheap

Old Woman:
cheap? man, you can call it cheap
I was too proud to ask the world and what the world gave me

you could put it in your eye and it wouldn't make you cry
I know what's a bargain and I know what's cheap
and I don't need to buy from you
so you can pour away your drop of pain
pour away your drop of pain
pour out your whatchamacallit panacea
spill your goddam thingumajig pharmacopeia
throw away your top hat frock coat cane
you don't know how it is with me

Umlaut:

I am Umlaut, Madam!
and you insult me, Madam!
you disparage, defame, reject, humiliate and shame me, Madam!

for I am Doctor Umlaut the paragon!
Doctor Umlaut the automaton!
I am seated at the feet
of the Tetragrammaton!

Old Woman:

man, man, those are fine words
like angels with trombones
like cherubim with swords

but will you take my hand? and
will you walk with me?
will you lead me to Beulah-land

I am so lonely, man
I am so lonely, man
I am so lonely, lonely, lonely, man

I live in a room where the walls press in
upon my twisted bones upon my shrivelled skin
I got as old and ugly as a body can
but you don't know how much uglier it is than sin
to be so lonely, lonely, man

Clockseller:
don't make me go

Broom-girl:
will you be there, to touch my hair

Umlaut:
I come home at night and lay down my staff

Old Woman *(softly)*
I am so lonely, man

Umlaut:
turn the radio on
and hear the voices calling down the winds

I heat up my supper left from yesterday
smoke my cigar, drink my beer

look in the mirror
comb out my beard and count the grey

Old Woman:
I am so lonely, man

Umlaut:
when I take off my clothes I see that I am
only a piece of the flesh that is known as a man
but I reach for the light as well as I can
toward the light as well as I can

brothers and sisters, there's time to cast away stones
time to gather stones together
to consider love and giving
not to talk about the weather in the sky

Alto:
brothers and sisters, let me testify
that we turn and turn again
to the pain of other days
vanity of vanities
sowing vineyards in the seas

Tenor:
the fool holds his hands and eats his heart
and hates the light
and the wise all their lives
turn their breasts toward the knives
and their hands toward each
other in the night

Soprano:
and the warmth between their bodies blesses
all the world of light
the world of light

WORDS FOR AN IMAGINARY FUTURE

Tom Marshall

Anne:

A dream is a wandering
in the body. The self descends
into itself. The psyche becomes
world.

　　　If you want to
understand me you must
know my body
is sometimes a house
and sometimes a landscape.

The landscape contains
the house
and the house contains
three sleepers
three dreamers
whose wandering perplexes
me because it contains
everything and nothing
that I am.

John:

I had a dream
last night, it was strange
and ludicrous:
from under the bathroom
door water is seeping. Inside
everything is smashed

glass, marble. . .
Then I awoke.

Anne:

That is a "house" dream.

Patrick:

In *my* dream there is more
suspense.

Anne:

      Tell it then.

Patrick:

                I will. First
there is a hand that
reaches out to me
from mounds of rubble
left by some war,
a disembodied hand
reaches out to me and
I dare not take it.
It is a naked man —
puny, coloured green —
who climbs
slowly and (I think) painfully
from under a tremendous hill
of refuse, tin
cans, tires, the anguish
of glazed bottles and bewilderment of burnt
shells of cars.

          Then
there was a great wind
and he grew, gradually,
very large until he filled
the whole sky
there was a green sky

but then
the wind subsided and
I cannot remember
what was to happen. . .

Anne:

Your dream is a landscape
almost realized.

        Someone
has said somewhere:
"The things of the night
are not the same
as the things of the day."

Patrick:

Aren't they? Today, travelling here,
I noticed, as always,
the discontinuity of things,
objects defined
by random areas of light
that separate themselves
from the larger dark.

I thought back then to
how our lives contracted
those years ago in
brief spaces of light
so brilliant we could not
bear it, being cowards. . .

Anne:

It was very
ordinary, really.

A wind off the lake made
gull-cries sound
right outside the door.
Clouds were moving in the sky

and I remember
that before we left
the rain stopped.

Patrick:

The huge limestone
churches standing firm,
the blind earth receiving the rain,
what could that mean
to the cloistered
skylit attic
where we lay

our radiant bodies moving
in the sun-capped clouds,
your first ecstatic
cries so quickly drowned
amid the magnificent
whirling anthems
of triumphant gulls?

John:

Love is versatile.
Love fades like a chameleon
into love.
Ice cracks and blurs
on the night streets that are
full of ghosts.

In bed
we become ourselves again
no longer ghosts.
(And yet I partake now
of that other whom
I resemble and do not resemble.)

Anne:

Lately I am able
to read both your minds.

I know your separate versions
of our intricate histories.
Together we might become
true. As it is
we are not genuine dreamers
but only actors in the dream
of another.

John:

The dream encloses
and imprisons us.

There is no help
for it, and no way out.
In the dream I move
into a further room
only to see
your ghostly face
accuses me of love.
I am too strong
for you to break me
and too compassionate
to wholly break you
even when I want to.

Anne:

You are weak, really.
You are my husband.
I married you because
you were weak.
A house for my freedom.

Patrick:

How can a house
make you free?
I offered you the
endless spaces of my mind.

Anne:

You were my lover.
You enslaved me, gave
me endless landscapes
of fear, all
your claustrophobic
flat prairies, your
murderous
mind-mountains and black lakes.
Like Orpheus you descended
into those places that
would have drowned me.

Patrick:

Orpheus is a space-man
who structures space.

John:

Then he must have built
a house, been an architect
of something enclosed. . .

Patrick:

No. . .

John:

Yes. Enclosure. Focus:
these things are necessary
to a love or a landscape.
This woman chose me
and abandoned you.
Even when we were apart
we were together
moving inward like a divided eden.
Then we came together and
undertook our torment.

Anne:

The world fell away from us. I forgot
my other, older life
for a time.
I *was*
happy. But then
there came a certain
recklessness. The trees beckoned and the owls
reproved me. The bright gulls
cried outside
the cold glass of my happiness.
The window expanded
before my eyes
till the house became
transparent again. . .

John:

Then you were only used
images: the restless
incandescence of mist
in lamplight, a
cloud surrounding

the moon. Ice, candles
suggested you. A glowing
ghost blown in
with the blue snow.
Not real. But I

was fool enough to wish
unravelling of
your "silken cloud", your
gentle luminous layers
of atmosphere, and wished

waking of warmth
in green earth below.
A restless earth
crumbling away in
islands, a far-flung

archipelago of flesh
floating in shadow seas.
That was you
this morning. I stood
and stretched naked as if

yet in the proud
sanctuary of darkness.
I felt the resonant
anthems of my own
detached body. I saw
headlights, gold
parentheses swimming
into the dim frame
of awaking nakedness
we shared. You

were moving slightly
but seemed out of
your body. Outside the
window, turning, I saw
a white and yellow milktruck.

Patrick:

The *numinous milktruck!*
How ridiculous, how
petty your world is!

This woman chose you
and became restless.
What could you give her
beyond false security?

I remember
her mouth on me, leaves moving. . .

Anne:

I looked out and the houses
were gone. There was a great
wood and the land sloped
down gradually to the lake.

Oh, do you remember
how we built the cabin
with our own hands
of logs from that wood?

Patrick:

The brown men helped us.
That was another life.
A dream from which we awoke
in our separate rooms, in cities. . .

Anne:

There were no cities then
and no towns of consequence.

Patrick:

At night we observed the cool
planets, the shifting of
summer stars. Once
there was a great
light that hovered in the forest
like an omen.
It darted and shifted
in the trees
like a yellow swallow
then disappeared
instantly
leaving a great silence.
Sleep was absolute and
followed by morning.

Anne:

The smell of smoke in autumn
in the clearing. . .
Pale gold haze. . .

Patrick:

Slow rhythms of our
nights and days created
us. Does it matter
then whether this memory
is fantasy or truth?

The body's mind is a labyrinth
of islands, lakes and rivers.
It is itself both beast and thread.
It is our privilege
(since we are living)
to raise and purify the dead.

MUSICAL INTERLUDE

Anne:

Husband!
What are you thinking?
Where are you?

I've lost you.

John:

Lately it has occurred
to me that old cars
are cranky not because
they are decaying machines
but because they are
evolving very
slowly into organisms,
branching, establishing
circuits we cannot comprehend.

In their deserted automobile
graveyards they whisper at night
together, they meditate, mutter about
the mysteries of cybernetics,
the problem of rejection,
they plot, they plan quietly together
an ultimate and terrible day.

Anne:

You are moving away again.
I cannot follow you into such
a future as you describe.

John:

When I was a child I felt
my prophetic powers but could not
comprehend them.
I knew, however, that my father
could not really be
my father.
Hitler
was my father. I knew it
in my bones.
One day
before the war
was over
he would kidnap
my mother. I knew it.
I would then
have to kill him
in order to rescue her.

Anne:

I am losing you
to your fantasies.
Perhaps once in another
life you sailed
to Troy. But we are
here, now.

John:

But how did we come here
to this place
of snow and silence?
And where are we going?
When we met I was

a changeling
who wanted to become
human.

Anne:

Do you remember the time last
winter when we first
walked out
on the frozen lake?
How they saddened us, that
multitude, so many
brightly coloured skaters.

John:

It would take someone like Breughel
or Vermeer
to record it accurately:
all those figures moving in the vast expanse
of mellow light.
Like birds
(how conventional, but there you are),
like nothing so much as a flock
of dark seagulls.
Anonymous, but seeming enormously free.
Pouting their sails of unconcern
they circled and wheeled
like metaphors
whose only meaning is motion
floating the bright black and grey top
of their own weightless January mood
while behind them the misted
islands, a delicate backdrop,
were melting in the dull,
the diminishing glow
that fell heavily across the landscape.

Anne:

It is this last, marvellous, ochre glow
that burnishes the mild winter day, pleases
with the same illusion of well-being one gets

from a decent liqueur during a good dinner.
We appreciate the dulling
of our ordinary boredom,
the glaze that satisfies, and we look
idly at the single line that is horizon.

John:

And we are children without gaiety:
like children we slide and push
and scan the lake for omens, or perhaps
lost emotions.
We observe the ice today
is like stained glass done
with Canadian good taste:
rather like a big black and grey marble
stretched flat for miles;
a thick and variable child's mystery
full of lines, jagged cracks and grey mix;
a crystal ball revealing the occasional
frozen fish.

Anne:

And we laugh
as we observe the skaters in their low,
impossible light,
and we are children
without gaiety.

John:

It troubled us and so
we returned
to a house
that much more haunted.
Ghosts of the not-so-
distant past troubled us
as much as future ghosts.

Patrick:

I built the house with
mercury. Invisible logs,
whirling atomic
particles. It was you
closed into your fear
who lived there. Why
were you afraid?

John:

The great elm cut
down like a slain beast
by the courthouse (whale
or bear stretched
upon the vast waste
of snow above the park)
troubled me as waking
dreams troubled me.

The gates, the patched
white-and-green lawns
glowed strangely in the brief
hour of day's end. Sky
was green at one
end and peach-red beyond. . .

Anne:

                              Soon
the white glittering
anarchy of stars surrounded
us. It was then
our duty to rejoice.

It was the house that
shielded our winter love,
clothed our cold bones with laughter.
But **the spring** followed after.

Patrick:

Anna, Anna. . .

Now you must choose.
I have returned
from wandering
from necessary exile
to claim you. You must leave
these sheets of cruel snow. . .

John:

Cruel snow? On that ground
the snow
blossomed into strange
and lovely fevers
orchids of delight
the unfolding lotus
of our after-stillness. . .

We made our own spring
in that marriage-chamber.

Anne:

If I must choose then each of you
must help me to choose.
Each must speak his reasons which will be
my reasons.

MUSICAL INTERLUDE

John:

In chambers of spring
air and water
shimmer cool as cymbals.

In chambers of spring
gown and curtain
ripple green as glass.

In chambers of spring
moon and willow
waver pale as candles.

In chambers of spring
fire and wind
mingle bright as beads.

You who snared my love
in a smiling net of flame
come and lie with me
in the chambers of spring.

You who caught my joy
tight in curls of cloudy gold
come and lie with me
in the chambers of spring.

You who fixed desire fast
in eyes quivering arrow green
come and lie with me
in the chambers of spring.

MUSICAL INTERLUDE

Patrick:

Two nights before I flew back to Canada I dreamed about the house—*the*
house, the model for all others, three-storied, huge and old to the child that
looked at it from under the heavy-branched lilac-tree, pleasantly ugly in its
formal, Victorian sprawl, solid in confidence—only in the dream it had
become a skeleton, a frame, naked to the wind and the night rain, and I was
balanced on the outer top beam, precarious, moving along by inches, one
foot after the other, edging slowly along the left side of the house, which was
swaying a little now and creaking in the wind, then along the back beam, and
then forward along the right side, till I came, inevitably, to the children,
without surprise or foreknowledge, and they looked up at me for a moment
from some absorbing game, Mark, my brother, with the beautiful face, his
large dark eyes and black hair, and beside him, a little smaller, myself, *about
six*, I thought, plumper, with indeterminate brown-coloured hair and lumpy,
less defined features, then Eric who looked just like Mark and was now

somehow the same age instead of eight years younger, then a stranger with red hair, freckles, and *this is my friend Jimmy* said Mark, so we all laughed, because there had never been any such person, it was just a joke, and I wondered later that I had not, in this dream, met or remembered my mother, but that somewhere in the dark warm house I knew my father lay sleeping, filling the place with his protective presence, so that the invisible rhythms of his sleeping body, his huge, recumbant frame, flowed into it, and extended even beyond it until the fierce wind was his breathing.

MUSICAL INTERLUDE

Anne:

I walked down the hill
one morning through the welcoming green
trees. Bits of wildlife were busy
about me. Squirrels and bluejays
observed me. When I reached
the glittering waters I removed
all my clothes, all my old
disguises. The brown, the green
man reached gently to take me
into his canoe. We moved then
steadily and surely toward
the thousand islands that awaited us.

THE END

GARDENS OF THE WIND

Alden Nowlan

First Voice:
The daisies are growing through the eye sockets of the skull.
They reach up for the sun
as everything that lives
reaches up for the sun.
                       (Even vegetables go crazy
in blind cellars, the paranoid potatoes
sprouting mad tentacles that grope towards a light
they can neither foresee nor remember.)

The daisies are growing through the eye sockets of the skull.

If we had discovered this sooner
we'd have gathered stones
                       of a particular
shape
     and colour
and piled them one on top of the other.
We'd have played shepherds' pipes
and beaten drums.
                    We'd have linked hands
with strangers
             and danced
                as flames dance,
leaping
     higher and higher.

Sound: *Marching drum beats — quick march — background for following:*

Second Voice:

The engineers have come into our fields.
They do not make paths and keep to them
but walk where they please, trampling the grain.
Their grins are lordly; they wear
mysterious hats and boots.

The engineers have come into our pastures.
They are city-bred and have never learned
the importance of gates,
                              so cattle and sheep
roam the roads.
                    Old men who give
names to the years
                         will remember this
as the year the animals
raided the vegetable gardens.
                         Yes, they will say,
that was the same year
the war started. Every sunset
was the colour of blood, they'll say,
barns were struck by lightning
and the cattle—
                    the cattle everywhere
broke out and raided the gardens.
That was the year
the war started.

Third Voice:

The engineers
have come into our yards.
They pump water and drink from our wells
without performing the small but necessary
ceremonies.
              They do not knock at the door
and agree it is hot,
                    hotter
than it was yesterday,
                         hotter
than they hope it will be

tomorrow or the day after.
                    The woman watches them
from her kitchen window, standing
far back from the glass
and slightly to one side.
                    Their laughter is lordly.
They peer through their instruments
and send messages to one another
with their arms.
                    Their hands
are gloved in soft leather.
They drive
        stakes in the earth.

First Voice:

And one old man
tears out the stakes
and burns them.
One old man.

Second Voice:

What was it the old nut kept yelling?

Third Voice:

Damned if I know, It sounded like:
Thou shalt not crucify the land.

Sound: *Judge's gavel*

Fourth Voice:

Oyez. Oyez. Oyez.
The charge against the said
is that he did knowingly,
wilfully and with
malice aforethought
remove and destroy
an unspecified number
of wooden stakes,
the property of
Our Lord the King—

Voices:
God save the King!

Fourth Voice:
—and did thereby
give aid
and comfort
to the enemy—

Voices:
Frustrate their knavish tricks!

Third Voice:
Hang the son of a bitch!

Fourth Voice:
—and did also endanger
our national sovereignty
and territorial
integrity, did, in short,
offend
against his God,
         his King
            and his Country.

Music: *O Canada—few bars*

First Voice:

The wind has no love
for the trees,
        yet there is grass growing
in the wounds of the elm,
twelve feet from the ground. Who
but the wind
could have made such gardens?

Second Voice: *(To be read seriously, not as parody.)*
We shall fight them on the beaches
and on the landing grounds.

We shall fight them in the hills
and in the streets.
We shall fight on and on,
and we shall never surrender.

Third Voice: *(To be read seriously, not as parody.)*

If I advance, follow me.
If I die, avenge me.
If I retreat, kill me.

First Voice:

The boulder cannot see the rain
whose fingers it has directed
for so many thousands of years
that now there is a hollow
in the stone

      and there, too,

           the wind has planted.

Sound: *SEIG HEIL! SEIG HEIL! SEIG HEIL!*
          (Incidentally, the following is the Italian Fascist cheer.)

Sound: *EIA EIA EIA ALALA! EIA EIA EIA ALALA!*

Third Voice: *Hail, Caesar! We who are about to die, salute you.*

Fourth Voice:

And the Lord God of Israel poured out His wrath
upon the Jebusites.

First Voice

One day

      so far from now
that only the most learned men
will care whether or not
our civilization
ever existed,

      one day the grass
will crack open
this rock

     like an apple.

Sound: *Military drum: quick march: background for following:*

Second Voice:

The caterpillar men have come into our fields.
Their machines are like the knives of fishermen
that slit open the bellies of trout.
The caterpillar men have come into our fields,
the caterpillar men and the dynamite men
have come into our fields,
into our pastures,
into our yards.

          The dynamite men have come into our fields;
and the glass in the windows

                      trembles;

the spoons on the table,

                 the knives and the forks

rattle against the plates;

             the cups and saucers

mill about,

        chattering;

             the very house

shivers almost
        as a man shivers
when his teeth
        are set on edge.

Third Voice:

The dynamite men have taken over our land.

First Voice:

The plow is husband to the earth.
The earth is a woman

            and the plowshare

                  a phallus.

Sound: *Judge's gavel*

Fourth Voice:

Prisoner, what is your name?

First Voice:

I lived here before God was born,
before he called back
the innumerable separate particles of himself,
before the god-spark flew out
of everything that lived,

               and the sky was full
of small bright bits of God returning
to rejoin his body.

             I wonder how many
millions of eagles
it took to make his eyes, and how long he waited
for the soul of the great tree that became
a single hair on his smallest finger.

Sound: *Derisive laughter silenced by Gavel*

Fourth Voice:
Prisoner, how do you plead?

Third Voice:
There is no order
               except that
which the mind confers:
               the small boy exploring
the swamp,
        tasting the mystery
of the orchid,
       the only one
               ever found there,
part of the apocrypha
               of one man's life,
the miraculous
           infancy of us all,
the small boy
             contemplating the orchid,
and, of course, he becomes
a prince reared by swineherds

for fear of his uncle,
the usurper,

        but there is more to it,

                much more,

the small boy contemplating the orchid
for days

      or weeks

          or months

             · or years

                  or centuries

—the beginning of a myth.

           There is no order

except that

      which the mind confers.

              There is no order—

Sound: *Derisive laughter interrupted by drum roll and*
                       trumpets fanfare

Fourth Voice:

Prisoner, I heartily wish it were in my power to
                sentence you
to be hanged, disembowelled and castrated—

Sound: *Vigorous applause and cheering*

Fourth Voice:

Since, unfortunately, that is impossible, it is
              my order that
you be returned to the house from whence you came,
              there to be
afflicted by the ridicule and resentment of
            your family, your
friends and your neighbours until such time as
            it shall please
God to terminate your existence—

Sound: *More applause and cheering.*

Fourth Voice:

—And may God have mercy upon your soul!

Music: *RCAF march past*

Third Voice:

And now the local news.
Wednesday, January 25, 1940.
Five months ago, Michael David O'Sullivan, a
                        76-year-old
farmer battled with the RCAF and lost.
O'Sullivan removed and destroyed surveyors'
                        stakes and at
one point threatened government officials with
                        a rifle, in
the course of his attempts to prevent the
                        expropriation
of his land as site for an RCAF Flying Training
                        School.
Ironically, O'Sullivan was buried in the family
                        cemetery,
less than one hundred yards from a runway that
                        covers what
was once a pasture for his cattle.
I have just been handed a bulletin. Marshal
                        Petain today—

Sound: *Roar of Second World War Aircraft*

Second Voice:

Yet, they were beautiful in their way, the planes.
Butter-coloured, they were, swarming like bees.

First Voice:

Or like palomino colts,
                leaping
from cloud to cloud.
             Yes,

they were
        beautiful.

Fourth Voice:
And they were ours.

Third Voice:
Ours.

Second Voice: *(diminishing)*
Ours.
    Ours.
        Ours.

Sound: *Planes gradually rising*

Third Voice:
We were all children.
There were Norwegians,
Australians, New Zealanders,
Poles, Frenchmen,
Englishmen, Canadians,
and wild back-thumping,
chest punching,
rebel-yelling
Texan irregulars.

Sound: *Planes reach crescendo and out.*

First Voice:
We were all children.

Second Voice:
We were all children.
        They wore blue tunics,
the colour of the sky before a summer rain,
and wedge hats,
      and sometimes

there were pistols on their hips,
and a few of them patrolled
the tall barbed wire fences
with rifles and bayonets.
                              We
went barefoot and almost naked
during the summer.

First Voice:
We were all children.

Third Voice:
Loving them,
                    we talked in their slang.

Second Voice:
Cheerio, old chap. Keep your pecker up. Smashing.

Third Voice:
He's a good old boy, you all. Hear?

Second Voice:
We said, "hello" and "goodbye"
in Norwegian and Polish.

Music: *"Beer barrel Polka" blend with "I've got sixpence"*
                                                    cut

Third Voice:
We were all children.
                          Aching
to grow taller,
                    knowing
when we grew tall enough
that we, too, could have wings
                          and fly.

Sound: *Sound of planes*

Second Voice:

When one of the student-pilots was killed
the flag on the hangar
was flown at half-staff.
We could see it clearly
from the schoolyard,
although separated from it
by a valley and a river.

       We pretended to grieve.

Sound: *Drum beats: Slow march: Out after third voice*

Third Voice:

We were all children.
      We pretended to grieve.
Knowing no name but "grief"
for the wonder we felt,
tasting the mystery.

Second Voice:

And, of course, we were envious.

Third Voice:

Yes, we envied them their death.

Second Voice:

In our dreams we saw them die
like lightning bolts thrown from the sky.

Third Voice:

The day the war ended,
the teacher told us
we could go home.
      We cheered ourselves sore.
And, afterwards,
     because the war was over
I went into the woods alone
and lay down in the moss
       and cried.

First Voice:

Grown men go to war
less because they want to kill
than because
they desire to die.

Third Voice:

I went into the woods alone
and lay down in the moss
                         and cried.

First Voice:

There is no order
               except that
which the mind confers.
There was the star that fell
by daylight,
          and the boy was afraid
to tell even those who sat
in the same room with him.
                            It happened that
he glanced at the window
an instant before
it struck the earth,
               a great wheel of flame
fallen
     from the chariot of heaven,
a crescendo
      of sparks
              in the backyard,
the ordinary
            backyard
where he had played
for as long
        as he could
              remember,
and he never afterwards
looked for evidence
of its fall.
        To touch the world
with the most private
parts of self,
          to find

a child's dreams
encompass history.
                    That
is the lost
key to the circle.

Sound: *Buildings being wrecked behind following:*

Second Voice:

The destroyers have come
        with their Morning Stars,
                with their iron pendulums.
The destroyers have come
        with their sledge hammers and fire axes
                —the nails scream
                as they're torn from the wood.

 Third Voice:

The barracks are gone.
The mess halls are gone.
The hangars are gone.

 Second Voice:

The earth has made no provision
        for the works of man.
Concrete does not grow with the rain,
        nor does the sun
                        strengthen it.
Everything that lives
        is in league with the grass.

 Third Voice:

In the cold,
        the crust
                of the earth
stirs
    like the flesh
                of a woman,
shivering.

Second Voice:

The concrete gives way.

Third Voice:

The sun
        opens it
                like a flower.

Second Voice:

And grass
grows in the wounds.

First Voice:

Who but the wind
could have made
                such gardens?

Third Voice:

The daisies are growing through the eye sockets
                                of the skull.

Sound: *Judge's gavel.*

Fourth Voice:

Prisoner, what is your name?